T0368505

PRAISING *GOD* *in* *the* NATIONAL PARKS

The Four Corner States

Addison Doyle

WestBow Press books may be ordered through booksellers or by contacting:

WestBow Press
A Division of Thomas Nelson & Zondervan
1663 Liberty Drive
Bloomington, IN 47403
www.westbowpress.com
844-714-3454

All photos by the author.

English Standard Version (ESV)
The Holy Bible, English Standard Version. ESV® Text Edition: 2016. Copyright © 2001
by Crossway Bibles, a publishing ministry of Good News Publishers.

ISBN: 979-8-3850-3707-0 (sc)
ISBN: 979-8-3850-3706-3 (e)

Library of Congress Control Number: 2024922613

Print information available on the last page.

WestBow Press rev. date: 11/18/2024

WestBow
PRESS®
A DIVISION OF THOMAS NELSON
& ZONDERVAN

Addison Doyle

This book is dedicated firstly to my mom who not only has encouraged me

to follow my dreams of visiting all the national parks, but has traveled

with me to each and every one and shares my adventurous heart.

To my dad, who shares my passion for planning, is a great travel companion,

and willingly holds down the fort when Mom and I are gone.

Thank you, also, to the rest of my family and friends, who have

stood by my side and encouraged me to fulfill my dreams.

I love you all!

Table of Contents

Introduction

It is He who made the earth by His power,
Who established the world by His wisdom,
And by His understanding stretched out the heavens.
Jeremiah 10:12

There is proof of a loving God who created the whole world and all of nature around us. We see evidence of God's hand in everything from a gnat to an elephant, from a rock to a mountain. There is just something incredibly special about looking down into what seems like a never-ending canyon, observing my surroundings from the edge of a mountain, standing under a naturally made arch, and seeing only cacti for miles and miles. Every time I go to a different national park I see God's wondrous work and am able to separate myself from the stress and anxiety of everyday life and to instead focus on God's beauty around me. This is why I have made a goal for myself to travel to all the national parks. Not only to see God's marvelous creation, but to give myself that needed time to really separate myself from the busyness of this world and just be surrounded by God's handiwork.

As I have slowly made my way across the United States, I have encountered something very troubling in our national parks. The signs you read in the parks mainly describe formations as being millions of years old or point out rivers that shaped a canyon over the span of hundreds of thousands of years, flowing upstream at that. These claims frustrate me because they only state one side of the argument (evolutionary naturalism) and they don't give people the chance to consider creator was and still is at work. My starting point for understanding the world around me is Genesis, which proclaims that God created all in 6, 24-hour days, and therefore supports a young earth worldview. It is very troubling to me that the literature provided at the parks assumes a naturalistic agenda without considering creation as a viable perspective and reality. This book is for everyone who chooses to marvel at the beauty of a national park through the lens of creation science. As I walked through amazing landscapes I knew I disagreed with evolutionary explanations, but wasn't totally sure how to describe what I was seeing in scientific terms. I found myself wishing for a young-earth, creation-science perspective because I knew one existed. I could give broad-stroke answers such as, there was a worldwide flood which had something to do with it, but I wanted to know more and be able to put it into words to combat what I was reading, sign after sign. I jumped right in and started doing my own research on Biblical worldview explanations for how the parks were formed, are preserved, and do continue to change. I hope this book excites readers and park-goers to challenge the park-sign claims, do some reading and research, and marvel at the parks through a Biblical lens. Hopefully this book encourages readers to experience the national parks through the eyes of a Christian worldview that celebrates scientific discovery. Yes… the Bible and science work perfectly together!

I wrote a short devotion to go along with each national park so that, if you are like me and feel close to God in nature, you can use the opportunity to give God the glory before, during, and after your visit to the park. For each park, I will include some notes from my own experience, favorite hikes, safety precautions, and, of course, some pictures! Bring this book with you on your adventures, read it with your family, friends, and fellow adventurous spirits and please enjoy each of these four corner national parks as much as I have.

Arizona

Grand Canyon National Park

For his invisible attributes, namely, his eternal power and divine nature,

have been clearly perceived, ever since the creation of the world, in the

things that have been made. So they are without excuse.

Romans 1:20

I have been to Grand Canyon National Park four times now, but each time I experienced my surroundings entirely differently. I was very young the first two times I visited the Grand Canyon, but there are two key things that I still remember to this day. One was looking over the edge of the canyon and thinking about how dangerous everything looked. There were donkeys walking on the edge of the cliff, the sun glistened off the sunburnt necks of hikers, and I feared the possibility of falling into the canyon myself. I was scared of my surroundings and yet amazed, not only by the beauty of the canyon, but also by the complexity of it all. The third time I visited the national park was with my entire family and participated in one of the Canyon Ministries tours. Our tour guide took us all around the canyon and explained what we were seeing through a Biblical worldview to include the effects of the flood described in Genesis. We were looking at the beauty that came out of the sorrowful flood. This was the moment I knew I wanted to make sure the world could hear everything I just heard, but from all parts of the United States. I was forever a different person after this tour and looked at nature through a new set of eyes. The most recent time I was at the Grand Canyon was just this past year. I took mom for Mother's Day and to take notes on the future book that I was hoping to write (you are reading it now). It was wonderful to be able to circle back to the place that sparked the idea for this book in the first place. Everything has a start and a finish except… God, who is never-ending and never changing.

Devotion: The Grand Canyon is not only a national park, but one of the seven wonders of the world. The world has acknowledged the wonder of the Grand Canyon. Have you ever noticed that the Grand Canyon has Bible verses all around the park? This is because the Evangelical Sisterhood of Mary believed that this national park was a gift from God and decided to post Bible verses all around the park to honor Him. Up until the modern era, many people believed in God and saw this national park as an example of His marvelous creation. Now, there are attempts to have the scripture verses removed. How do we as Christians protect not only our history but also our values when the National Park Service wants to remove any reminders of what Christians believe? I hope this encourages you to stand firm in what you believe and feel comfortable honoring God in public. Consider reading the verses out loud with your travel companions or saying a prayer to the mighty God of creation. Praising God in public can go a long way and might just plant that seed of belief in someone who sees you respecting God's marvelous creation in this way. This is also a good reminder that people are watching and listening so we need to be honoring Christ through our actions and how we treat people as well: "Little children, let us not love in word or talk but in deed and in truth" (1 John 3:18).

Science: It is said that the Colorado River carved the Grand Canyon. Have you ever considered that a river might not be able to carve a canyon this big? The Grand Canyon is 277 miles long, 18 miles wide, and 1 mile deep with a total of 1,904 square miles in total. That is a big canyon! It's time to think from a different perspective and determine what seems the most realistic. From a creationist point of view, we look at the Grand Canyon and know that the worldwide flood from the Bible is what carved this humongous canyon. Some people might already know what I mean when I talk about the worldwide flood and others might not so here is a quick overview of the account (or read Genesis chapter 6-9). Many years after the fall of Adam (when sin came into the world), God saw how corrupt the world was and decided to flood the world to destroy the immense evil of humankind. God warned everyone through His trusted believer, Noah, and provided opportunities for repentance and escape, but none besides Noah and his family turned from evil to God. So God commanded Noah to build an ark before He flooded the world. Noah's family and 2 of every type of animal (so they could reproduce) were spared. The worldwide flood was sudden and quick which also explains why scientists have found fossils that were buried mid-run or even while giving birth. This quick burial explains the fossil record with more credibility than the naturalistic argument of a river carving the canyon over millions of years. You also have to wonder why there are no signs of erosion. There are tens of thousands of feet of sedimentary layers, of which about 4,500 feet are exposed in the walls of the Grand Canyon. If the thickness of sediments was deposited over 500 million years then some boundaries between layers should show evidence of erosion. You should also wonder why each bedrock layer is totally flat if they were exposed for millions of years, as claimed by evolutionary naturalists. Each layer of bedrock is flat because another layer immediately went right on top of it during the flood ("Grand Canyon Facts"). There are nine major sedimentary layers seen at the Grand Canyon and these layers are exposed for all to see. Tom Vail says it perfectly in his book: *Grand Canyon: A Different View*: "If you examine the geology of the Grand Canyon with an open mind, I believe you will see how the evidence points to a young earth". The Grand Canyon not only proves God's existence, but also proclaims the reality of a global flood. The way of escape through the ark demonstrates His mercy and points toward humanity's escape from sin and death through salvation earned by Jesus Christ.

Trails and Tips:

Trails:

- Kaibab Trail: This trail is 7 miles down to Phantom Ranch which is at the bottom of the canyon. I recommend hiking down this trail in the early morning and staying at Phantom Ranch for the night. The next day hike back up the canyon but on the Bright Angel Trail (listed below). If you only want to do a short day hike then I recommend hiking to Ooh Aah Point, which is the beginning section of Kaibab Trail, and then back up (1.8 miles round trip).

- Bright Angel Trail: This trail is 10 miles from the bottom of the canyon back to the top (or vice versa). This trail is more gradual then the Kaibab Trail and that is why it is recommended to go back up from the bottom of the canyon.

Tips:

- Purchase *Your Guide to the Grand Canyon* here: https://answersingenesis.org/store/ product/your-guide-grand-canyon/?sku=10-2-335 for a more detailed guide book on a creationist point of view on how the Grand Canyon was created or click here: https://www.canyonministries.org/tours/ to look into an in-person tour at the Grand Canyon through the eyes of a creation scientist.

- If you are planning on staying inside the Grand Canyon at one of the lodges you need to plan at least 12 months in advance. The lodge at the bottom of the Grand Canyon is lottery based so make sure you apply. If you are hoping to go with a group, have everyone do a separate lottery entry for better odds. If you don't get it the first time, keep trying. Consider being flexible with your dates or try for an off-peak time.

- If you are visiting the Grand Canyon in the summer remember to bring sunscreen as the temperature can get as high as 120 degrees and most of the trails are in direct sunlight.

- The Grand Canyon is one of the seven wonders of the world and the second most visited national park in the United States. Be prepared for crowds.

- Watch out for Moose that cross the road! I speak from experience.

Saguaro National Park

For everything created by God is good, and nothing is to be
rejected if it is received with thanksgiving.
1 Timothy 4:4

I was so excited to find out that there was a national park only two hours away from my home in Phoenix. Mom and I could now plan a fun day trip to Tucson and back. I got out all my national park books and started doing research on the park to make my game plan. I started reading about the national park and it seemed everything was about the cactus family - hence the name of the park. I kept thinking, "why is this a national park? We see cacti all the time!" Once I started to really think about it though I realized that the Saguaro was a rare plant that only grows in very specific locations in the US. This national park was perhaps not a brand new landscape for me to behold, but it is a stunning, majestic, and new environment for most visitors. Thinking about how visitors less familiar with the mighty Saguaro might experience the park helped me maintain a sense of wonder. I learned an important lesson to always keep an open mind and be willing to look at things through the eyes of someone else. This mindset can help us appreciate the beauty and uniqueness of others (true of humans and plants!).

Devotion: Have you ever been pricked by a cactus? It isn't fun, right? There are many different types of cacti and they all seem to have nasty spikes! There are Jumping Cacti, Barrel Cacti, and Saguaros just to name a few. Cacti seem to only be good at one thing though and that is pricking us with their sharp thorns. What is so special about cacti when all they do is hurt us? When we think this way we need to remember that God created cacti as well and nothing that God created should ever be rejected. The spiky cactus doesn't necessarily want to harm us, but it has thorns because it needs to protect itself from critters. Sometimes we are like a cactus in that we put up a wall to protect us from the harmful words and actions that people send our way. Sometimes we even feel tempted to spout off harmful words at others which makes me think of a jumping cactus so easily attaching its painful thorns to passersby. We need to remember that all of God's creation, including each of us, have faults we might use to hurt someone else, but that doesn't mean we are rejected. In fact, God does the exact opposite and continues to love us no matter the mistakes we make. Thank you, God, for giving us this reminder through your prickly creation.

Science: Saguaros thrive in only a few very specific areas in the Southwest including Arizona and part of Mexico. This type of cactus is very rare and that is why they are taken care of and protected in Saguaro National Park. This national park acts as a sanctuary for the Saguaro in an attempt to protect what little we have left of this majestic species. There are estimated to be about 1.8 million Saguaros in this national park, but every year the number goes down due to harsh weather conditions. Saguaros can grow to be 50 feet tall and weigh more than 2 tons, but they don't grow their first arm until they are 50-70 years of age. Saguaros also offer food and shelter to over a hundred other plants and also animals and continue to be the iconic picture of the desert ("Saguaro"). One of the main questions people have about saguaros is if you had to, could you drink the water inside of them? The answer is you should probably not drink the water from inside a saguaro cactus. Why? It is very acidic and will most likely just upset your stomach. That said, the Gilded Flicker and Gila woodpecker find the Saguaro a perfectly protective house. The Saguaro is an incredible plant that is so unique and different from any other plant and its uniqueness helps prove that it did not evolve from a different plant or animal. The Saguaro is unlike any other plant in that it can store up to a thousand gallons of water, has flowers that only bloom for as little as one day, and protects itself with thousands of spikes. God has created an amazing plant that helps prove his majesty and power.

Trails and Tips:

Trails:

- Desert Discovery Nature Trail (0.5m): This is a self-guided nature trail with signs along the way. It is very easy and family friendly.

- Valley View Overlook Trail (1m): This is a short, easy walk that puts you right up next to some Saguaros. This trail ends with an amazing viewpoint that looks out over thousands of Saguaros.
- Signal Hill Trail (0.3m): a short trail that has some elevation gain towards the end. This trail is a must do because along the way you see petroglyphs that were created by the Hohokam people.

Tips:

- The scenic drive has a lot of potholes and is not kept up very well. Make sure to drive slowly or put your car in 4-wheel drive.
- There are not many trail options, so you probably won't need more than one day to tour around this national park unless you plan on backpacking (you will need a permit to backpack).
- There are a lot of wasps and bumble bees so if you are allergic make sure you bring your epi-pen.

Petrified Forest National Park

Though its root grow old in the earth,

and its stump die in the soil,

yet at the scent of water it will bud

and put out branches like a young plant.

Job 14:8-9

This was the first national park that we took the boys (my younger brothers) while having my book in mind. They were troopers and did all the hikes and went to all the viewpoints with me. It was riveting to see the national park through their eyes and to have them experience something that is so important to me. I had a blast getting to teach them about the national park, my passion for visiting all the parks, and how they were now a big part of my journey. Finding beauty in a corrupt world is a trade that I have now passed on to the younger generation. Perhaps they will share this book with their future families and introduce others to the excitement of seeing God in the beauty of these marvelous places.

Devotion: Everyone and everything grows old with time. Did you know that the Petrified Forest used to be a full grown, thriving forest with loads of vegetation? We all grow old with time and eventually die, but we know that we will go on to be in heaven if we believe that Jesus Christ is our Lord and Savior who died on the cross for our sins. When Christ comes again our bodies will be perfected and in heaven there is no sin or sorrow. The petrified trees remind us of this because they used to be young trees once and then they died, but it didn't end there! They were crystalized and are now even more strong and beautiful. While just an earthly example, when looking at petrified trees we can think ahead to the eternal truth that the best is yet to come! Just like the petrified trees have become something better after death, so eventually will we based on the promises of Philippians 3:20-21: "But our citizenship is in heaven, and from it we await a Savior, the Lord Jesus Christ, who will transform our lowly body to be like his glorious body, by the power that enables him even to subject all things to himself" (Philippians 3:20-21).

Science: The number one question that people ask about this national park is how did the Petrified Forest become petrified? Did it used to be a lush green forest? If you were to ask a park ranger or read one of those signs at the national park it would tell you that the forest was buried by large and quick amounts of water and sediment millions of years ago and the trees slowly decayed creating the petrified wood and fossils. Well, I'm going to give you another way to look at it. The Bible talks about a flood (about 5,000 years ago) that covered the entire face of the earth (Wright, David). The worldwide flood covered this forest and all the animals that lived here in water and sediment and this explains not only the petrified wood we see today, but also the fossils. While under water, the wood absorbed minerals and created a crystalized layer inside the wood. When the flood waters went down, people could see what we see today: petrified wood. Dr. Snelling in his description of the aftermath of the flood wrote, "Many of the logs are oriented in the same direction, testifying to the rapid water currents that carried them with the sediments in which they were then buried." Petrified wood is wood that has been reformed into a crystalized rock. This entire national park shows the beauty of these crystals all over the desert groundscape.

Fun fact: Did you know that petrified wood is the state fossil of Arizona ("Arizona Facts")?

Trails and Tips

Trails:

- Blue Mesa Trail (1m): This trail is a loop through the Blue Mesas. The path is paved, but towards the end the trail goes straight up and there is a large elevation gain. Many list this as the #1 thing to do in Petrified Forest National Park.

- Crystal Forest (.8m): This trail shows off some of the best crystalized petrified wood in the park.

- Giant Logs (.4m): Visitors are able to see a petrified log that is almost 10 feet in diameter.

- Long Logs/Agate House (2.6m): See some petrified logs that are still intact and also an old Pueblo house built from petrified wood.

Tips:

- Bring a hat and sunscreen if you visit the national park in the summer time because all of the trails are in direct sunlight.

- It's recommended to stay in Flagstaff for the night and make the 90-minute drive to the national park rather than stay in the area directly surrounding the park.

Utah

Zion National Park

"How lovely is your dwelling place, O Lord of hosts! My soul longs, yes, faints for the courts of the Lord; my heart and flesh sing for joy to the living God. Even the sparrow finds a home, and the swallow a nest for herself, where she may lay her young, at your alters, O Lord of hosts, my King and my God. Blessed are those who dwell in your house, ever singing your praise! Blessed are those whose strength is in you, in whose heart are the highways to Zion."

Psalm 84:1-5

Have you ever felt like if you close your eyes you might miss something? That describes my entire experience at Zion National Park. It started out with hunting for a parking spot. My eyes were glued to the car window trying to find somewhere for us to start our adventure. I didn't dare blink an eye. Finally something caught the corner of my eye… A parking spot! Except, I wasn't sure it was a *full* parking spot. We took our chances and squeezed into this half of a parking spot on the edge of a cliff. Shortly after carefully stepping out of the car we jumped on the shuttle and once again glued our eyes to the window as we passed mountains and canyons that had seemingly invisible tops. Once we finally started walking we really had to keep an eye out for other people's feet due to the tremendous number of people on the trails. When we got to a point on the trail where it was just us and the mountains we could finally see the beauty of this national park and appreciate its magnitude and why so many people take time to visit it. Visiting this national park is like seeing a piece of heaven, which is why it is so amazing that "Zion" is a word to describe heaven in the Bible: "But you have come to Mount Zion, to the city of the living God, the heavenly Jerusalem. You have come to thousands upon thousands of angels in joyful assembly" (Hebrews 12:22).

Devotion: Have you ever wondered how Zion National Park got its name? If you are familiar with the Bible then you know that Zion is mentioned in the bible to describe heaven. When the Mormon settlers came to this area of Southern Utah they thought it was a perfect representation of what Heaven, or "Zion" in the Bible, might look like. There are also three peaks that the Mormons named The Three Patriarchs after Abraham, Issac, and Jacob in the national park. Zion is a place like no other and that is probably why the early settlers wanted to name it after Heaven. Have you ever noticed how much nicer everyone seems in the national parks? People are smiling, they are sharing advice, they make room for more park-goers to hop on the shuttle, and most just have a general air of excitement. I believe it is because everyone has the sense that they are in God's creation (even if they don't want to admit it) and the miracle of God's creation can be felt and is visible everywhere you look. I feel closest to God when I am standing in the midst of His wonderful creation and I can imagine that others feel this way as well. In Luke chapter 19 we read that, "He answered, 'I tell you, if these were silent, the very stones would cry out.'" I like to describe places like Zion National Park as the most beautiful of *rock* symphonies and that people who are visiting are enjoying the beautiful visual harmonies and melodies in every direction they look. To add to the experience, consider playing "In The Garden" (https://www.youtube.com/watch?v=3_dMzucjEaw) as you do the scenic drive through Zion and let your praise cry out to the God of the universe.

Science: Zion National Park is known for its steep cliffs, plants and animals, the Virgin River that winds its way through the park, and so much more. How did this canyon come into existence? First we will take a look at what evolutionists want us to believe and compare it to the creationist point of view. The signs and the rangers will tell you that the Virgin River carved out the canyon and left a small river in its place. A different possibility, based on a young earth explanation, is that Zion's landscape was carved out by a worldwide flood, the same one that shaped the Grand Canyon. The second option lines up with the historical account of the Bible. It makes much more sense that there was one large flood thousands of years ago that covered and forever changed the earth. Zion Canyon is 2,400 feet deep and 15 miles long (Yogerst, Joe). Which is easier to conceive as mighty enough to carve out such a canyon: a skinny river or a raging, worldwide flood? Yet, books, signs, and even rangers speak of the river theory as if they were there and it was captured on a go-pro camera. To figure out which argument seems stronger we look back in history to compare similar canyons and their history. Do some reading about the documented Mount St. Helen's eruption that happened in 1980. Most remember the main eruption, but not everyone recalls or discusses another discovery as a result of that event. After the eruption a deep canyon, about one-fortieth the size of the Grand Canyon, was found. This canyon was formed by the force and momentum of the mudflow from the eruption and it was formed in just one day! Just think about how much greater was the impact of a 40-day worldwide flood. Does this help you accept and embrace that a massive canyon, like Zion, is not the result of a skinny river? Rather, it is from the explosion of water the Bible describes in Genesis 7:11 this way: "In the six hundredth year of Noah's life, in the second month, on the seventeenth day of the month, on that day all the fountains of the great deep burst forth, and the windows of the heavens were opened." Furthermore, there is now a small flowing stream that goes right through Mount St. Helens Canyon and this mirrors the Virgin River that now flows through Zion. Had the Mount St. Helens eruption not happened in our lifetime, scientists would probably have assumed that another skinny river of water carved the canyon over a span of millions of years. Yet we know the eruption happened in our lifetime! Mount St. Helens is one of many historical events that proves the young earth theory.

Trails and Tips:

Trails:

- Emerald Pools (3m): This trail is unpaved and goes through the mountain to a secret oasis. The first pool is the Lower Emerald Pool and there is a small waterfall you walk under and are able to feel the spray of the water as you walk underneath it (in the summer). You then continue on to the Middle and Upper Pools. The hike becomes more strenuous, but it is well worth it in the end!

- Riverside Walk/Narrows (2.2m-10m): The Riverside Walk is a 2.2m round trip paved trail that ends right before you have to cross the stream to continue on to the Narrows. You will be able to see the hanging gardens on the Riverside Walk. The Narrows takes you on an additional 7.8m hike once you cross the stream.

- Angels Landing (5.4m): Angels Landing is the most popular hike in the park. To be able to complete this entire trail you must have a permit to hike beyond a certain point because it can get dangerously busy. This is a very steep hike with many switchbacks, but the view at the top is incredible.

Tips:

- Grab the first parking spot you see! Zion National Park is known to have thousands of visitors a day so it can be difficult to find a spot to park. Once you find a parking spot you need to find a shuttle stop as you will want to travel by shuttle to most of the trailheads. If you can not find a parking spot, drive the Zion-Mt. Carmel scenic highway first and then try again for a parking spot.
- The GyPSy app is a great addition to have on this trip if you want to learn some interesting facts about your surroundings. If you choose to purchase the app, remember to bring earbuds so you can listen as you ride on the shuttle. However, similar to the park signs, the narrator sadly describes formations and rock as millions of years old. If you choose to use this app with young children you should definitely be proactive and explain that the narrator is sharing an opinion, NOT fact.
- To be able to hike Angels Landing you will need to get a permit at recreation.gov.
- If you plan to swim or soak: There are specific rules about which pools and areas of water are safe to swim in so make sure you ask a ranger at the visitor center.
- Take binoculars so you can look at the magnificent layers and colors in the mountains.
- If you are visiting Zion National Park and Bryce Canyon National Park take the Utah Scenic Byway 12 which connects the two parks. It's a beautiful drive!

Bryce Canyon National Park

I will give you the treasures of darkness
and the hoards in secret places,
that you may know that it is I, the LORD,
the God of Israel, who call you by your name.
Isaiah 45:3

I wanted to do everything that this park had to offer. Something about this place made me feel that there was no concept of time and I could keep walking on and on with time seeming like it was standing still. We hiked to every possible viewpoint and explored every area but I still felt like I needed to see more. Hiking into the "canyon" was breathtaking and shocking while hiking back out was incredibly rewarding. When the time came to eat lunch we were able to sit out in the sun, something Arizonans rarely can do, and chow down on our rice cake sandwiches. Nothing could have made this day more perfect and an idea to plan a National Park trip every September took root. September – the month of comfortable sunshine and endless walks, the possibility of fewer visitors due to school being in session, not to mention the potential of great travel prices and deals. Try planning your next trip in September!

Devotion: Have you ever seen something so incredible it confirmed your belief that there has to be a creator? Bryce Canyon National Park is one of those places and is like a secret treasure that God has gifted us. There is nothing on earth like this place… a deep gorge filled with hoodoos! What are hoodoos? Hold that thought; we will get into that in the science section. God has gifted us with treasures all around the world, but they are not always appreciated in the right way. We need to be better about thanking God for the gifts he has blessed us with. I'm not just talking about the wonderful national parks now, but also the people He put in our lives for very specific reasons, or the opportunities He lays out in front of us. God is all around us; we can see His touch through our lives and the marvelous creation with which He has gifted us. "'Am I a God at hand, declares the Lord, and not a God far away? Can a man hide himself in secret places so that I cannot see him? declares the Lord. Do I not fill heaven and earth?' declares the Lord" (Jeremiah 23:23-24). When you look at the incredible and unique formations at Bryce Canyon, give thanks to God for His amazing gifts, the greatest of all being His Son, Jesus, our Savior!

Science: What are hoodoos and how were they made? Hoodoos are the narrow spires of rock that you see rising up out the Bryce Canyon's amphitheaters. Hoodoos are created by erosion, rain, and wind from freezes and can grow to be 200 feet tall. Evolutionists believe that the hoodoos were formed under water and then tectonic force pushed up the columns which exposed them to erosion millions of years ago. It is true that the columns were created and lifted by water, but not millions of years ago. About 5,000 years ago there was a worldwide flood (yes, the same one mentioned in the above chapters) that carved the plateau at Bryce Canyon and also chiseled the hoodoos. The flood water then forced the hoodoos up and they were exposed to erosion. These spires of rock were chiseled into what they are now from the weather, specifically the winter. In the span of just one year there are more than 200 freeze-thaw events that take place at Bryce Canyon National Park. So, how do the hoodoos not just crumble and break? The rock at the bottom of the tower is actually softer than the rock at the top which protects the tops of hoodoos from future erosion (Snelling, Dr. Andrew A.) Another big question that visitors have is whether Bryce Canyon is really a canyon? The answer is no. Bryce Canyon is a plateau, but was given the "canyon" name because traveling pioneers would call it that through word of mouth. The name ended up sticking and it has been called a canyon ever since.

Fun fact: Did you know that Bryce Amphitheater contains the largest amount of hoodoos in the world?

Trails and Tips:

Trails:

- Rim Trail (5.5m): Connects some of the most popular viewpoints (Inspiration, Sunrise, and Sunset) in the park.

- Navajo Trail and Queen's Gardens (3m): This is a 3-mile loop that starts at Sunrise point (Queen's Garden) and ends at Sunset Point (Navajo Trail). Along this loop you will see Thor's Hammer, Queen Victoria, and the Two-Bridges.

Tips:

- Bring a jacket, even in the summer, as it gets cold down in the canyon. But don't be surprised if you take the jacket on and off as you walk at different elevations.

- There is a great parking lot, just to the left of the visitor center, if the visitor center is full. The shuttle then picks you up at the visitor center and stops at most of the viewpoints and trails. The shuttle is not required, but recommended.

Capitol Reef National Park

The mountains rose, the valleys sank down
to the place that you appointed for them
Psalm 104:8

Total silence. There was no one here except us and nature. I closed my eyes and felt the cold breeze on my skin and the sunshine on my face. Many times we think of silence as a time of solitude, but it can also be an orchestra of sound. You just have to be willing to pause and train your ear to listen. Silence is one of the most beautiful orchestral arrangements and the composer is Jesus Christ. I love to picture Him directing the sounds of silence from on top of the clouds knowing that those who take a moment to pause and listen in the silence are blessed with their own personal concert. This national park is not high on most people's bucket lists and because of that it is one of the least visited national parks. People see this as a reason to not bother visiting, but I see it as an opportunity to hear God's musical masterpiece. The experience I had at this national park has trained me to hear the beauty in silence and feel God's presence through the wind.

Devotion: Capitol Reef National Park is one of the few parks that doesn't have any accommodations like hotels, gas stations, and stores near it. This national park is authentic and out in the boonies! Because of this, not many visit this national park making the visitation rate much lower than Zion National Park and other more popular park destinations. Sometimes it's necessary to be forced into seclusion so that we can really appreciate and feel God's presence around us in His creation. I loved being able to hear the wind blowing around me, the sounds of animals a distance away, and to stare up at the cliff walls and see God in everything. God is literally in everything and to see His handiwork up close and personal is a gift we could never repay. Speaking of gifts, God not only gave us marvelous things to look at, but the gift of salvation. God gave up His one and only son to die for us on the cross and because of this we are saved and have the promise of eternal life. When we believe in Jesus, we go to heaven, a place where there is no sorrow or sadness: "He will wipe away every tear from their eyes, and death shall be no more, neither shall there be mourning, nor crying, nor pain anymore, for the former things have passed away" (Revelation 21:4). When I'm surrounded by the majesty of a National Park it feels like a tiny glimpse of Heaven.

Science: The #1 question that people ask when visiting Capitol Reef National Park is why is it called "capitol reef" when the surrounding environment is all desert and mountains? The mountains in this national park are very unique in that the top and bottom part of the mountains are distinctly different. The top is smooth and pointy while the bottom looks almost like a popcorn ceiling. The national park got its name from settlers who thought the white domes looked like the capitol building and they thought the bottom portion of the mountains looked like a coral reef. They combined the two and thought up "Capitol Reef."

In truth, the portion that looks like a popcorn ceiling is the part that was pushed out from the ground during the worldwide flood ("Geology"). Knowing that the unique features are a result of the flood, I like to think that another explanation for calling the park, Capitol Reef, is a nod to the waters that rose up and came down during the flood. Less than 5,000 years ago, at the time of the worldwide flood, the water pressure was so strong that it pushed the mountains up: "The mountains rose, the valleys sank down to the place that you appointed for them" (Psalm 104:8).

Another portion of the national park that is a must see is the "swiss cheese" as it is informally called. The cheese-like holes are actually called potholes or "pockets" because they are holes in the mountain walls. Created by seasonal rains, these pockets provide a home for the creatures that live here during the rainy season and hot summers.

Trails and Tips:

Trails:

- Capitol Gorge Trail (5.5m): A trail that goes through the canyon and gives spectacular views of the canyon walls and the "swiss cheese."

- Cassidy Arch (3.6): This trail is named after Butch Cassidy, the famous outlaw who hid out in the remote area. This is a very strenuous hike so make sure to bring water and take lots of breaks.

- Hickman Bridge (1.8m): A moderate trail that features a natural 133 foot bridge and wonderful canyon views.

Tips:

- Don't plan on going to this national park in the rainy season as many of the trails wash out and flood making them inaccessible for vehicles.

- This national park is in the middle of nowhere so make sure you investigate places to fuel up and stock up on water and snacks well in advance.

- The trails are marked by rock cairns, or poop emojis (too much information?) as my family likes to call them. Follow the rock cairns to stay on the trail. Park rangers request that you do not build additional ones.

Arches National Park

For you are my rock and my fortress;

and for your name's sake you lead me and guide me

Psalm 31:3

Arches National Park is in my top three national parks so far visited (I have visited 39 national parks as of this book being published). The diversity and beauty of these arches is unlike anything I have ever seen. If I were to recommend a national park to someone this would be my first recommendation! At one moment you are looking at an arch where you can't even see the top, then an arch inside a sand cave, and another that is so long that it looks like it could break in pieces any day. I was giddy with excitement at every turn and could not wait for the next adventurous trail. I felt rejuvenated and ready to head back to the "real world" after being able to experience such magnitude. The day ended with us driving out of the park and seeing the billions of stars in the sky. I was born and raised in the city and had never seen anything quite like the starlit sky above Arches National Park. I will never forget this park and will always remember my child-like excitement over its magnificence.

Devotion: Arches National Park is full of incredible arches, each truly a marvel to behold. The arches need a firm foundation or they will cave in or crumble. Speaking of that, there is an arch, Wall Arch, where chunks have fallen off or crumbled. God tells us in the Bible that we need to have Him and His word as our foundation. God is our rock and fortress and without Him our foundation starts to crumble just like Wall Arch: "Everyone then who hears these words of mine and does them will be like a wise man who built his house on the rock. And the rain fell, and the floods came, and the winds blew and beat on that house, but it did not fall, because it had been founded on the rock" (Matthew 7:24-25). We need to remember that no matter what we are going through in life we can always go to God's word to see what God has to say and to be strengthened by His promises.

Prayer is also an important part of keeping our foundation strong. Let's pray; Dear God, please help us to enjoy our time in Arches National Park. Help up also to see the crumbling arches as a reminder of why we need to strengthen our lives with your word. Please keep our foundation strong and stable through You. We know that you are truly our rock and fortress. Amen.

Science: Arches National Park has more than 2,000 natural arches, including the world's longest arch at 89 meters long. How is it possible that these arches are not man made? How were they created then? If you were to read the signs in the national park they would tell you that it was millions of years of erosion acting on the sandstone layers. In reality these arches were created by more than just gouged holes in sandstone rock walls. In the article, "Arches of Utah", we learn that Arches National Park sits on underground salt beds which are not stable. Arches are the remains of sandstone deposited on top of the salt beds. When the sandstone was left on the salt floor, the weight caused the salt to liquify and force itself up which pushed up the sandstone creating fins (sandstone rock walls). Wind and rain helped shape the sandstone walls, or in some cases, deteriorate the middle/bottom portion of these walls, creating arches. This leads to the question of how do these arches not cave in? The article continued to explain that when it rains or water collects at the bottom of these arches it causes the bottom to weather more quickly creating a stronger base. However, these arches will not last forever and are already starting to crumble before our eyes. Who knows how long the world's longest arch will be at Arches National Park, so go and see it before it's gone!

"Forty-three arches have collapsed due to erosion since 1970. Their loss is a sober reminder of how delicate—and recent—these formations are. Rapid processes created them and are now destroying them" (Snelling, Dr. Andrew A).

Trails and Tips:

Trails:

- Most of the Arches National Park trails are off of the scenic drive that goes through the entire national park. Some of the best stopping points and little trails are Balance Rock (0.3m), Tunnel Arch, Windows and Turret Arch, Pine Tree Arch, Double Arch, Landscape Arch (1.6m), Skyline Arch (0.4m), Sand-Dune Arch (0.3m), and Pothole Arch. There are many other arches to see with over 2,000 arches in the national park, but these are a few of my favorites.

- Delicate Arch Trail (3m): Delicate Arch is the arch on all the Utah license plates. This is a must do if the time permits.

- Sand-Dune Arch, pictured below, was one of my favorites. Remember your camera! Oh, and be ready to remove your shoes (you'll see what I mean!).

Tips:

- Arches National Park requires timed entry and a small fee (visit recreation.gov) to be able to enter the park during "business" hours. Make sure to do this if you plan on coming to Arches National Park anytime between 7am and 4pm.

- All of the trails are stops along the scenic drive so be prepared to stop frequently.

- This national park is very busy during the day time and becomes more open around 5pm. I also recommend coming late or returning to the park to see the stars. Arches National Park is an international dark sky park.

Canyonlands National Park

By awesome deeds you answer us with righteousness,

O God of our salvation, the hope of all the ends of the earth

and of the farthest seas; the one who by his strength established the mountains,

being girded with might; so that those who dwell at the ends of the earth are in awe at your signs.

You make the going out of the morning and the evening to shout for joy.

Psalm 65:5-6; 8

Somehow we ended up at the right place at the right time. It was 7am and we were walking to our first destination - Mesa Arch. Little did we know we were headed to a destination where the professional photographers wait for hours so they can get the perfect shot of the sunrise through the Mesa Arch. So like I mentioned before, we were blessed to be in the right place at the right time. In fact, the front cover of this book is a picture I took at this very moment when the sun was rising right through the arch opening. Though, some were not as lucky as we were! There were about 30 people set up with their cameras getting ready to get the perfect shot. When the sun finally rose enough to be seen through the arch someone broke through the crowd and took a picture of this beautiful scene, but while doing so, blocked everyone else! You can imagine the amount of anger and frustration that was present at this moment. What a chaotic start to the day! We were just so thankful to have witnessed the beauty of the sun peeking through the arch slit and to have caught the moment together.

Devotion: When standing on the edge of the canyon in Canyonlands National Park you can't help but be in awe of God's wonderful creation: "so that those who dwell at the ends of the earth are in awe at your signs. You make the going out in the morning and the evening to shout for joy" (Psalm 65:8). One of the most famous places to visit in this national park is Mesa Arch, a natural arch that is right on the canyon edge. This is the place that everyone flocks to, hoping to watch the sun rise through the arch opening. Seeing the beauty of the sunlight streaming through the arch is an amazing way to start the day with joy and anticipation. God wants us to start every day this way. How can we do this? We can wake up and do a devotion, praise God for His blessings, give thanks for the gift of a new day ahead, and marvel at the beauty of His creation. We are not limited by our location; in fact, we can have a joyful and thankful mindset whether watching the sun rise from the front porch or from the opening in Mesa Arch!

Science: Canyonlands National Park is huge! The park consists of 337,570 acres with the highest point being more than 7,000 ft above sea level ("Biophysical Description of Canyonlands National Park (U.S. National Park Service")). It is said that this national park was formed from erosion and that the Green and Colorado rivers carved out these canyons over millions of years. Now, doesn't this sound very familiar?! Well, I've got a familiar explanation as well. Almost 5,000 years ago there was a worldwide flood that carved out canyons and pushed up mountains. I know I have said this many times, but it's very important to remember this as it explains how many national landmarks and parks were formed. We are going to specifically look into a couple areas at this national park including Upheaval Dome, Island in the Sky, and Mesa Arch. Upheaval Dome is a geological wonder where rock layers look deformed and in the center there is a circular formation called a dome. Many believe that this dome was created by a meteorite that collided with earth millions of years ago, but was there anyone there millions of years ago to prove this? The answer to that is no. Creationists agree that it very well could have been a meteorite, but explain the event as having hit the earth thousands (not millions) of years ago. Island in the Sky is a mesa that rests on sandstone cliffs over 1000 ft. above surrounding terrain. This piece of land is connected to other surrounding terrain by one strip of land called "the neck." Creationists believe that this area of land, separated from all other terrain, was formed during the worldwide flood as well. The mesa was forced above the flood waters and now sits high above other areas of land. Mesa Arch is one of the biggest wonders at the park as it is an arch sitting right on the edge of the canyon walls. For more details and an explanation on how this arch was created, please revisit the science section in the chapter on Arches National Park. The worldwide flood forced up sandstone rock walls (fins) above the ground and weather conditions, over time, created a hole in the wall, forming an arch.

Trails and Tips:

Trails:

- Mesa Arch Trail (.6m): This trail is .8 miles round trip from the parking lot. It is a necessity especially if you are able to make it in time for the sunrise. Beware, this is such a popular event each day that visitors start to arrive and claim a spot well in advance of the sunrise. If you want an unobstructed photograph, get there plenty early!

- Whale Rock (.8m): This trail goes up the side of a sandstone dome and is very steep. The dome that you climb looks like a huge whale.

- Upheaval Dome Trail (.6): This trail is short, but steep. At the overlook you can see where something (perhaps a meteorite such as I mentioned above) caved in the canyon.

- Grand View Point (1.8m): A trail that follows the canyon edge and offers spectacular views of the canyon below.

Tips:

- Canyonlands National Park is split into four sections. If you plan on doing this National Park just for the day I recommend doing the Island in the Sky portion of the park.

- The trails are marked by rock cairns (or you know what my family likes to call them!). Follow the rock cairns and park rangers request that you do not build additional ones or tamper with existing ones.

Colorado

Mesa Verde National Park

"Enduring is your dwelling place,
and your nest is set in the rock."
Numbers 24:21b

Many think that Mesa Verde National Park is all about the cliff dwellings, petroglyphs, and the people that lived there. Well, I was happily surprised to see beautiful mountains, trails, and greenery, as well. Don't get me wrong, the cliff dwellings are stunning and complex, but the nature and environment are just as breathtaking. One of my favorite moments was hiking to the top of the summit on Point Lookout Trail and seeing the entire national park from one vantage point. Mom and I took a minute at the top to really take in our surroundings and God's beautiful creation that we had the pleasure of seeing. Not many people were on the trail because everyone was so focused on seeing the cliff dwellings that they forgot there was so much more to explore.

Devotion: Mesa Verde National Park preserves cliff dwellings that are strategically situated on the sides of the mountains. It's hard to imagine that people used to live in cliff dwellings and climb the mountains around them just to get home! It helps us to really be thankful for what we have around us, doesn't it? We have a roof over our heads, a private mailing address, the ability to drive to a grocery store, flushable toilets, and even safety from the elements. We need to not only remember to be thankful for these things, but also remember that complaining does not get us anywhere. God always provides. We tend to complain when the grocery store doesn't have what we want in stock, the driver in front of us is too slow, or our package is delivered a day late! It's important to remember what other people before us have gone through and be thankful for what God has given us. Something I am particularly thankful for is God's marvelous creation all around us and the ability to see National Parks. It is certainly easier for me to drive to the Mesa Verde cliff dwellings than it was for the original inhabitants to get back from a day of gathering food.

Science: Mesa Verde National Park is different from most of the national parks in that the highlights of this area are the cliff dwellings, which are man-made. How is it that the cliff dwellings were able to stay upright on the side of a mountain and for such a long period of time? Efforts on the part of the national park service have helped preserve the history and architecture of a people group that lived in the area a long time ago. The dwellings are falling apart and perishing like everything else on earth, so the national park service works hard to keep them intact and monitor the area for potential deterioration. Spruce Tree House cliff dwelling is an example of this deterioration, and the national park service has shut down all access to this cliff dwelling because of the threat of collapse. They are hoping to repair the cliff dwelling to keep it from further collapse, but until then it is closed to visitors. Another question many people ask is why did the Puebloans build their houses on the side of the mountain? There are many reasons. Firstly, the mountain protected their house from natural elements. Secondly, it made it more difficult for animals to invade. Thirdly, their houses were hidden from other tribes. Everything deteriorates in time because this earth was not meant to last forever. Jesus will come back to earth and make a new earth full of everyone who believes in Him.

Trails and Tips:

Trails:

- Point Lookout Trail (2.2m): This trailhead starts in the Morefield campground and is moderately difficult. This is the highest point in the park and has spectacular views.

- Petroglyph Point Trail (2.4m): This is the only place in the park to see petroglyphs. The entrance to this trail is by Spruce Tree Cliff House.

- Far View Sights (0.75m): Visit the Far View Sights to see where the Puebloans lived before they built cliff dwellings.

Tips:

- If you want to go into a cliff dwelling you need to make a reservation 15 days in advance at recreation.gov.

- If you enjoy camping, this national park is one of the best places to camp. The campsite has functioning toilets and sinks and is very well maintained. There is also a cafe and general store right next door.

Black Canyon of the Gunnison National Park

This is the message we have heard from him and proclaim to you, that God is light, and in him is no darkness at all. If we say we have fellowship with him while we walk in darkness, we lie and do not practice the truth. But if we walk in the light, as he is in the light, we have fellowship with one another, and the blood of Jesus his Son cleanses us from all sin. If we say we have no sin, we deceive ourselves, and the truth is not in us. If we confess our sins, he is faithful and just to forgive us our sins and to cleanse us from all unrighteousness.

1 John:5-9

This national park shocked me like no other! Of all the national parks in Colorado, this one is the least visited and you don't hear many people say "I just loved Black Canyon of the Gunnison National Park!" Well, I absolutely loved this national park and it is one of my favorite national parks, probably because not many talk about it, so I was very happily surprised. Looking into this incredibly deep canyon gave me a feeling like no other and I had goosebumps up and down my arms! Zion National Park, Everglades National Park, and Grand Canyon National Park are considered some of must-sees (which they absolutely are!), but there are so many of the lesser known parks that should be on that must-see list, as well.

Devotion: At Black Canyon of the Gunnison National Park, there is a portion of the canyon that only gets 33 minutes of sunlight a day. Can you imagine being in a state of darkness for basically the entirety of the day? Some people have denied God and have chosen to live in the darkness. But God is the light of the world and He lights up our hearts and lives through forgiveness and the promise of His love. Without Him, our lives are bleak and without purpose. We need His light to guide us along the right path: "Again Jesus spoke to them, saying, 'I am the light of the world. Whoever follows me will not walk in darkness, but will have the light of life'" (John 8:12). This park's dark canyon is a good reminder to us that because of Christ we don't have to live in darkness, not even for 33 minutes! God is the light of our world and this park is a great reminder of how much we need God's light.

Science: How did the cliffs in Black Canyon of the Gunnison come into existence? Let's dive right in by first talking about what you will hear and read when you go to this national park and compare it to the Christian perspective. The secular perspective is that about 30 million years ago volcanos on both sides of the mountain erupted and buried the area under volcanic rock. The Gunnison River then began flowing a couple million years later and over time this river cut a deep canyon in the volcanic rock creating Black Canyon of the Gunnison National Park. When you see the depth of this canyon you will know that there is no way a small river could have carved it out: "They rose greatly on the earth, and all the high mountains under the entire heavens were covered" (Genesis 11:19). Black Canyon of the Gunnison has some of the most stunning cliffs that I have ever seen. When I looked over the edge it only confirmed what I already knew; the world-wide flood mentioned in the Bible formed these amazing cliffs. If these cliffs (made up of basement rock) were here billions of years ago the basement rock would be full of cracks after years and years of earthquakes and other tectonic motions ("Gunnison's Black Canyon: The Flood Solves Mysterious Mission Time"). Another question many ask is how the Painted Wall cliff came to be. It is believed that there was volcanic rock that cooled and cracked under the pressure. When the forceful and extremely hot water creeped into the cracks it created a painted look on the cliff sides. Secularists believe this as well, but think that it happened over millions of years when creationists believe it happened a couple thousand years ago. You have the opportunity to see this beautiful Painted Wall at the Black Canyon of the Gunnison National Park, and when you do, give thanks for the promise that God will never again destroy the earth by flood (*The Institute for Creation Research*).

Trails and Tips:

Trails:

- Rock Point Overlook (0.4m): This overlook is a quick and easy trail. It leads to, in my opinion, the best views of the entire national park.
- Warner Point Trail (1.5m): Pickup a trail guide at the visitor center for this hike if you want to read about the area as you walk. At the end of the trail you will be able to enjoy the view of the Gunnison River and Black Canyon.
- Oak Flat Loop Trail (2m): This trail leads you to the bottom of the canyon and then back up to the top giving you the ability to see the entirety of the canyon wall. This trail begins near the visitor center.

Tips:

- Do everything you need to do on your devices before going into this national park as the cell service is very spotty.

- Most of the viewpoints require a short 0.2 mile walk to reach the overlook

- Poison Ivy grows near the banks of the Gunnison River, so be on the lookout!

Rocky Mountain National Park

"For the mountains may depart

and the hills be removed,

but my steadfast love shall not depart from you,

and my covenant of peace shall not be removed,"

says the LORD, *who has compassion on you.*

Isaiah 54:10

We visited Rocky Mountain National Park in the month of May, but there was still snow everywhere! You all know I'm an Arizona gal by now. I am used to the blistering dry heat for 8 out of 12 months of the year and would never imagine seeing snow in May. At this point I still did not have any hiking boots, so I had to take things slow as I saw many were slipping and sliding through the snow trying to see as much of the park as possible. There were a couple times I would fall, but laugh, and get right back up again. I learned my lesson though and this was the last national park I visited without any hiking boots! At one point, Mom and I stopped and sat on a bench to enjoy the scenery- which we usually don't do because we are always go, go, go in order to see and do as much as possible! That experience was a reminder for me to pause and enjoy the calm and the added joy that comes from pausing to notice the details. Our amazing God can be seen in and cares about the huge mountains but also the small details in each one of our lives: "Look at the birds of the air: they neither sow nor reap nor gather into barns, and yet your heavenly Father feeds them. Are you not of more value than they?" (Matthew 6:26).

Devotion: Rocky Mountain National Park has the highest continuous paved scenic drive in North America. You start down in a forested area, then you move upward through the park into the mountains, and lastly you reach an area called the tundra. The tundra is on the top of the mountains, reaching about 12,000 feet in elevation, where trees don't even grow because it's too cold. This scenic drive has so many different terrains and it's hard to believe that you are still driving on the same road! In the beginning, God created the world in six days and each day he made something different. It's hard to believe all of this wonderful creation was created in those six days. Only a marvelous and wonderful God could create something so beautiful. We should always remember to be thankful for all that God has gifted us throughout our lives. We go through different stages, perhaps move from place to place, or experience the awe of a new adventure around the bend. This scenic drive in the Rockies helps paint a picture of some of the terrains that God created and is a great reminder of the beauty that He creates in our lives as well as in nature. I see this national park not only as a gift and a reminder of God's great power, but also his love for us. God loves us so much that he has gifted us with this beautiful earth and with His Son, our Savior, who has redeemed us through His blood. God is so great!

Science: What makes the Rocky Mountains so special and different from any other typical mountain range? While most of the Rocky Mountains are located in Colorado, they are actually not contained to only this national park. The mountain range actually stretches from New Mexico to Washington. Let's take a moment to reflect once again on how mountains, like these, were created through Noah's worldwide flood. When the floodgates opened and God flooded the whole world because of sin, earth's crust shifted and cracked causing mountains to rise up above sea level. Like many other mountain ranges, the Rocky Mountains have rock layers that were deposited during and after the worldwide flood. Once the mountains rose, the water receded and went to create what we know now as rivers, oceans, and lakes: "they flowed over the mountains, they went down into the valleys, to the place you assigned for them" (Psalms 104:8). You can see rock layers as you hike these majestic mountains and notice the different fossils embedded in them ("Rocky Mountain National Park"). Have you ever wondered why there are fossils that are found in the act of running or eating? Or fossils that were found where it is obvious that the animal was giving birth? This is because the rock layers landed, formed, and solidified quickly - not over millions of years. It's important to look at the environment and surroundings with a clear mind and not believe everything someone tells us just because they call themselves a scientist. In truth, there are many wise and brilliant scientists who believe in the creation account and explain our current landscape through a Biblical worldview that includes a catastrophic worldwide flood. We can all study and understand science and rejoice at how science and the Bible work perfectly together because we worship the God of both!

Trails and Tips:

Trails:

- Tundra Communities Trail (1.2m): This trail starts at the very top of Trail Ridge Road. It is in "the Tundra" so the ecosystem is entirely different than what you might expect.

- Alberta Falls Trail - Bear Lake Trail (3m total): This trail is in the Bear Lake section of the national park.

WARNING: You need to have a separate timed entry ticket to be able to get into this portion of the national park. This trail first goes to Alberta Falls and can then loop back to the trailhead or you can continue on to Bear Lake, one of the most popular areas of the national park. Bear Lake is a stunning lake in the middle of the Rockies.

- Cub Lake (2.3m total): This is a favorite hike during the fall season. This hike is moderately challenging and has wonderful lake and mountain views.

Tips:

- The GyPSy app is a great addition to have on this trip if you want to learn some interesting facts about your surroundings! If you choose to do this then remember to bring earbuds so you can listen as you ride on the shuttle. Reminder: The narrator will most likely refer to things through an evolutionary perspective, so be ready to correct his "facts" if you are listening with children. Use the opportunity to discuss the Biblical worldview, instead!
- Rocky Mountains National Park has a timed entry system so, if you are planning on entering the park between 9am and 2pm, you need to make a reservation (and $2 payment) on recreation.gov. If you have a camping reservation, this counts as your timed entry and you can enter the park at any time.
- Bring your bear spray. There are definitely bears in the park and they usually come out in the early mornings or late evenings. Consider also buying a bear bell to hang on your backpack.
- Bring waterproof hiking shoes as there is snow all over the ground, typically until late June.

Great Sand Dunes National Park

Then shall the lame man leap like a deer,
and the tongue of the mute sing for joy.
For waters break forth in the wilderness,
and streams in the desert;
Isaiah 35:6

The line to get into this national park was so long. It seemed like everyone was trying to enjoy this beach-like park on their Sunday evening before heading back to work. When we finally got inside the park, a parking spot was incredibly hard to find and we ended up having to park on the side of the road far away from our first trailhead. Also, the rangers directing traffic were very rude, probably out of frustration with having to direct cars all day. It looked like things couldn't get any worse, but then mom lost her phone and we ended up walking all the way back to the car to see if we left it there… we did. When we finally got to the sand dunes we were shocked to see water at the base of them. It was an amazing sight, but we couldn't help but worry about wet feet and blisters. This national park taught us the importance of planning ahead and always having a buffer hour in case things don't go as planned. And if things don't go as planned then to not let that damper the wonderful experience you could have in God's marvelous creation.

Devotion: The Great Sand Dunes is literally a hidden oasis in the middle of nowhere. You can see the mountains from a distance and then BOOM you see the sand dunes at the feet of the mountains. Isaiah mentions something like this as he describes the handiwork of Jesus and the magnitude of the miracles he has performed and can perform. "Streams in the desert" is the perfect motto for this national park. The Great Sand Dunes National Park provides a visual for what this scripture passage describes. From the parking lot all you can see is the backdrop of mountain ranges and some trees, but once you walk through the trees you see the majesty of the unique sand dune landscape. There are not only sand dunes, but a creek that covers the sandy floor that surrounds the dunes. Many people come to this national park just to lay on the sand and imagine that this park is a beach. This national park is not a beach, but a hidden oasis that God has blessed us with. When we walked through the trees we were in awe of what was in front of us. After the giddiness wore off we started to panic because we did not bring a towel or water shoes and worried about blisters from having wet feet when we hiked the sand dunes (which were on the other side). We eventually decided to take off our shoes and socks when we crossed the creek. We almost decided to turn back out of frustration at ourselves for our lack of planning, but I'm so glad we ended up walking across because it was so worth it. This applies to our everyday lives as well because sometimes we have to get through the hard, frustrating, and unplanned things in life to appreciate the good all around or on the other side. This definitely applied to my mom and me as we were walking through the water, complaining about our feet getting wet, only to arrive on the other side, able to enjoy the splendor of the national park all around us.

Science: Everyone always has the same question when it comes to the sand dunes. How were the sand dunes formed and created? They were formed by many different elements, the main one being wind. The bodies of water from this area, like Medano Creek, brought in large amounts of sand and sediment. The wind then blew these large amounts of sand towards the Sangre de Cristo Mountains (the mountains behind the dunes), while opposing storm winds came from the opposite direction squeezing the sand together and creating the compact structure you see today: the sand dunes. Many scientists believe that this process took tens of thousands of years. But what is the young earth theory behind the creation of these ginormous dunes? When the worldwide flood was over there were not only mountains that rose up and valleys that were formed, but sand deposits, or sand dunes, that were left behind. Large amounts of sand were carried and placed in different places around the world, and this happens to be a place where a lot of sand was placed! While some believe the wind and elements created these dunes, young earth theorists believe that these elements preserve the dunes. You might, like me, wonder why humans are allowed to trample up and down the dunes, displacing sand with every step. It's because wind continues to tunnel through this valley and squeeze the sand together, virtually replacing the sand and keeping the dunes intact. If you end up hiking the sand dunes you will be able to experience intense winds, yet rest assured, your footprints will be filled back in and the dunes will be there for tomorrow's guests. It's important to remember that the worldwide flood did not only create mountains and valleys, but also made the way for other amazing sights such as the Great Sand Dunes ("Great Sand Dunes").

Trails and Tips:

Trails:

- High Dune (2.5m Round trip): If you plan on hiking the dunes, this is the one to do. Hiking in the sand is very difficult so plan on this hike taking at least 2 or 3 hours. This dune looks like the highest in the park from the parking lot, but really the Star Dune is the highest dune peak.

- Star Dune (6m+ round trip): Keep going past High Dune to reach Star Dune. A warning is that this dune has no marked trail so you will need to have a good sense of direction. Star Dune is the highest dune in North America.

- Enjoy Medano creek. This is the creek separating the parking lot and the sand dunes. Many visit this national park just for the beach vibe.

Tips:

- To be able to get to the sand dunes you have to walk through water. Either bring a spare towel to wipe your feet off or bring a pair of water shoes so you do not have wet shoes and socks.

- Bring plenty of water and sunscreen. There are no shady spots once you are hiking the dunes.

- Hiking in sand is very difficult so make sure you take lots of breaks as you climb up the sand dunes.

- There is no camping at the Great Sand Dunes National Park for vehicles that don't have four wheel drive, so the closest place to camp if you do not have four-wheel drive is Zapata Falls (about 20 minutes from the national park).

- Don't forget your sled! There are some impressive drops that provide opportunities for a great ride. But just remember… you have to walk back up!
- This national park is very busy on the weekends because many visitors just come for the water at the foot of the sand dunes. Make sure to grab the first parking spot available!
- To be able to do the second half of the scenic drive you will need to have an automobile that has four-wheel drive.

New Mexico

White Sands National Park

How precious to me are your thoughts, O God!

How vast is the sum of them!

If I would count them, they are more than the sand.

I awake, and I am still with you.

Psalm 139:17-18

White Sands National Park was not what I was expecting it to be. All of a sudden there was snow-like powdery white sand everywhere. It was like a winter wonderland, except I was sweating. I was so thankful for the soft sand. In fact, it was much easier to hike in than the brittle sand from Great Sand Dunes National Park. Admittedly, we did not plan ahead to bring a sled to Great Sand Dunes, so we made sure to have one with us when visiting White Sands! Alas, the sledding did not work well in White Sands National Park, partly due to smaller hills and mostly because of the powdery consistency of the sand. Another difference, but one that worked in our favor, was that there were not many people around and we had most of the park to ourselves! A fun fact is that White Sands is 31st on the list of visited parks ("Most Visited National Parks in the US"). The high-traffic parks are such for a reason, but sometimes the parks with fewer people can have an appeal because of the ability to see fewer humans and more nature. It was amazing to be able to experience such a masterpiece of God's creation, just the two of us. Love you mama!

Devotion: In the Bible God talks about sand many times: "I will surely bless you, and I will surely multiply your offspring as the stars of heaven and as the sand that is on the seashore. And your offspring shall possess the gate of his enemies" (Genesis 22:17) and "How precious to me are your thoughts, O God! How vast is the sum of them! If I would count them, they are more than the sand. I awake, and I am still with you" (Psalm 139:17-18). These are just a couple examples. Sand is very fine and tiny and it's hard to imagine how many specks of sand make up a sand dune, yet God promised Abraham in Genesis 22 that he would have as many offspring as there is sand. That is a lot of offspring! God never breaks His promises though and Abraham had a son, Issac, and through Issac many generations were born, including God's Son, Jesus Christ, born of a virgin. When I look at sand I remember that God always stays true to His Word and will always be with us: "fear not, for I am with you; be not dismayed, for I am your God; I will strengthen you, I will help you, I will uphold you with my righteous right hand" (Isaiah 41:10). Next time you go to the beach, visit White Sands National Park, or even look at a sandbox, remember that God is always with us and thinking about us and never goes back on His word.

Science: Why is the sand at White Sands National Park white? The white sands are formed from a mineral called gypsum. Gypsum is formed when sand meets evaporated bodies of water ("Sand"). Gypsum is an extremely rare mineral, so it is incredible that there are mounds, or dunes, that are made purely from this substance. Another question that many ask about this national park is why people are allowed to just walk around on this rare mineral? And how does all the sand stay in this one area? The white sand stays in this one place because of the moisture left on the ground. As mentioned before, evaporated water helps form this mineral and the moisture from the water then keeps the sand in place. It would make sense then that during dry seasons the white sand would be in danger of blowing away, but similar to Great Sand Dunes National Park in Colorado there are two mountain ranges (the San Andres and Sacramento mountains) that help tunnel the wind in a way that keeps the sand in this one place. For this reason, people are able to walk on the sand without worrying that it will be disrupted to the point of ruining the habitat. In many parks, the signs say to stay on the paths, so enjoy the ability to wander and make your own path through the sand!

Trails and Tips:

Trails:

- Playa Trail (.5m): This trail gives you the first close up view of the white sands.

- Dune Life Nature Trail (1.5m): This was my favorite trail as you are hiking through the sand and are able to see how the desert ecosystem and white sand meet together. (See the picture below for an example of a tree that sprouted up through the sand.)

- Interdune Boardwalk (.5m): This trail goes through the white sands, but on a "boardwalk," so it is good for anyone that might have a hard time walking on sand. This trail has many informative signs as well.

Tips:

- I visited this national park during the winter season (February) and it was still hot, so I can only imagine how hot it is in the summer. Remember to bring lots of water, sunscreen, sunglasses, and a hat.

- On certain days of the year, White Sands National Park is closed due to military tests. Double check your schedule and plan around closure dates. You can check the schedule here: https://www.nps.gov/whsa/planyourvisit/park-closures.htm

- Feel free to bring a sled with you, but if you just came from Great Sand Dunes, don't expect the same thrill!

Carlsbad Caverns National Park

Trust in the LORD with all your heart,
and do not lean on your own understanding.
In all your ways acknowledge him,
and he will make straight your paths.
Proverbs 3:5-6

By the time we got to Carlsbad Caverns National Park we were ten minutes from the time listed on our timed entry ticket. Both mom and I were stressed about getting to our destination in time. Of course, we made it, but just in the nick of time! We practically ran down the trail into the caverns due to adrenaline and excitement. As you might guess by looking at the picture, the amount of light and the surroundings changed quickly. The temperature dropped considerably, it was extremely dark, and there were bats flying around overhead.

We were astounded by the sudden changes and so glad we made it in time to experience descending down into the cavern. While we were down in the cavern we saw so many different and fascinating rock formations and structures. When we finished exploring the cavern we decided to hike straight back up instead of taking the elevators. As we were hiking back up many people encouraged us, but thought we were going out of our minds to do something so difficult when there was a much easier alternative. Sometimes the easier option isn't always the best option. In the end, we were so glad to have taken the trail back up because we saw so much more due to the fact that our eyes had adjusted.

Devotion: When first starting the trail that goes down into the caverns I couldn't help but be a little nervous. All I could see was a big black hole in the earth and I was going to walk right into it. Walking into this dark cavern was nerve racking, especially since I couldn't even see my feet as my eyes had not yet adjusted to the darkness! But after about ten minutes I started to see things more clearly. I could see the trail in front of me, the beautiful rock formations around me, and other people walking in front or behind me. Sometimes our faith walk can be similar to this situation. We don't always know where we are going in life, what God has planned for us, or even if we are on the right path. We can't always see the path God has laid out for us, but we need to trust God. Sometimes it might take a while for our eyes to adjust to our surroundings and be able to see the beautiful plan that God has laid out for us. Sometimes this can be in hindsight, similar to climbing back out of the cave. Our eyes had adjusted and we were able to see things we had missed the first time. God will never forsake or leave us in a place of darkness because he is the light that guides our path.

Science: What is the difference between a cavern and a cave? A cavern is actually a type of cave that tends to have different kinds of rock formations. Carlsbad Caverns National Park is a unique cave system that has beautiful cave formations and also many different species including bats. So how was this cave formed? Caves such as this are formed by rainwater dissolving the limestone creating crevices that grow bigger and bigger ("Cave/Karst Systems").

Evolutionists believe that this takes millions of years because it would have to take a lot of water to dissolve that much limestone. But wouldn't it make more sense if there was a huge body of water involved? That maybe there was a global flood (that would sure be a lot of water) that helped dissolve the limestone quickly creating caves such as this? Another thing that interests many visitors is the many bats that inhabit this cave. Bats are such a great example of God's handiwork and even go as far as disproving evolution: "The bat is one of the few mammals that have something to do with flying and the only one that took flying to the bird level" (Hume). The author continues, "It impossible to believe that some mouse-like individuals were getting wing-like limbs by mutation and the 'wings' were growing out accompanied with the knowledge of how the 'wings' can actually be used" (Hume). Animals like the bat are one of many great examples of God's design and help prove that man-made theories do not work when trying to describe God's masterwork.

Fun Fact: The Big Room in Carlsbad Caverns National Park is the biggest cave chamber, by volume, in North America.

Trails and Tips:

Trails:

- Natural Entrance Trail (1.2m): This trail leads you down into the caverns and at the end there are restrooms and a set of elevators.

- Big Room Trail (1.3m): This trail is down in the caverns and begins at the rest area at the foot of the natural entrance trail. You will see some incredible rock formations along Big Room Trail.

* When you are done exploring the caverns you can choose to take the elevators back up or hike right back up Natural Entrance Trail to, just that, the entrance of the cavern. This will add another 1.2 miles to your total hike.

Tips:

- Bring a flashlight! When you are just starting to descend into the caverns it is very dark (I could not see my feet). It took my eyes a good ten minutes to adjust to the darkness and my headlight/flashlight was very helpful when all I could see was darkness.
    - If you choose to walk back up (instead of taking the elevators), make sure to look at your surroundings and you will notice things you didn't notice on your way down due to your eyes having fully adjusted to the darkness.

- To be able to walk into the caverns you have to have a reservation (timed entry). You can secure your reservation up to one month in advance and it is necessary to be able to enter the cave.

- Consider taking some distance as well as very up-close pictures in order to remember the overall look of the formations as well as the textures and details, which change drastically, along the way.

Sources

Admin. "Most Visited National Parks in the US." *National Park*, 6 Sept. 2024, www.national-park.com/most-visited-national-parks-in-the-us/.

"Arizona Facts." Office of the Arizona Governor, 3 Sept. 2020, azgovernor.gov/governor/arizona-facts#:~:text=Petrified%20wood%20was%20designated%20the,mountain%20ranges%20in%20central%20Arizona.

"Biophysical Description of Canyonlands National Park (U.S. National Park Service)." *National Parks Service*, U.S. Department of the Interior, www.nps.gov/im/ncpn/bpd-cany.htm#:~:text=Canyonlands%20National%20Park%20has%20been,the%20Green%20and%20Colorado%20rivers. Accessed 19 Sept. 2024.

"Cave / Karst Systems." *National Parks Service*, U.S. Department of the Interior, www.nps.gov/cave/learn/nature/cave.htm. Accessed 1 Mar. 2024.

"Geology." *National Parks Service*, U.S. Department of the Interior, home.nps.gov/care/learn/nature/geology.htm. Accessed 26 June 2024.

"Grand Canyon Facts." *Answers in Genesis*, answersingenesis.org/geology/grand-canyon-facts/. Accessed 9 Aug. 2023.

"Great Sand Dunes." *Answers in Genesis*, answersingenesis.org/kids/kids-feedback/great-sand-dunes/. Accessed 13 Sept. 2024.

"Gunnison's Black Canyon: The Flood Solves Mysterious Missing Time." *The Institute for Creation Research*, www.icr.org/article/gunnison-black-canyon-flood-solves-mysterious-time. Accessed 18 Dec. 2023.

Hume, Desmond, et al. "Is the Theory of Evolution Being Disproved by Bats?" *Biology Stack Exchange*, 1 June 1958, biology.stackexchange.com/questions/3097/is-the-theory-of-evolution-being-disproved-by-bats.

"Rocky Mountain National Park." *Answers in Genesis*, answersingenesis.org/creation-vacations/rocky-mountain-national-park/. Accessed 21 Jan. 2024.

"Saguaro." *National Parks Service*, U.S. Department of the Interior, www.nps.gov/sagu/learn/nature/saguaro.htm#:~:text=Saguaro%20National%20Park%20is%20home%20to%20over%202%20million%20saguaros. Accessed 19 Sept. 2024.

"Sand." *National Parks Service*, U.S. Department of the Interior, www.nps.gov/whsa/learn/sand.htm. Accessed 1 Mar. 2024.

Snelling, Dr. Andrew A. "Arches of Utah." *Answers in Genesis*, Answers In Genesis, 22 July 2018, answersingenesis.org/geology/natural-features/arches-utah/.

Snelling, Dr. Andrew A. "Hoodoos of Bryce Canyon." *Answers in Genesis*, Answers In Genesis, 29 July 2018, answersingenesis.org/geology/natural-features/hoodoos-bryce-canyon/.

Snelling, Dr. Andrew A. "Petrified Forest National Park- Painting a Different Picture." Answers in Genesis, Answers In Genesis, 15 Mar. 2023, answersingenesis.org/geology/catastrophism/pe trified-forest-national-park-painting-a-different- picture/?srsltid=AfmBOoFTJSF6qzCbYE2ZSsI5n GOTcf1lK9IyBI3zluBSXBCcw28h69G.

Vail, Tom. *Grand Canyon: A Different View.* Master Books, 2003.

Wright, David. "Timeline for the Flood." Answers in Genesis, Answers In Genesis, 30 Aug. 2024, answersingenesis.org/bible-timeline/timeline-for-the-flood/.

Yogerst, Joe. "Everything to Know about Zion National Park." *Travel*, 24 June 2024, www.nationalgeographic.com/travel/national-parks/article/zion-national-park.

About the Author

Addison was born in Southern California, but grew up in and calls Arizona home. She works on the ministry staff at Christ Church Lutheran and teaches piano to over 40 students. Some of her favorite hobbies include playing the piano, reading, spending time with her family, and of course hiking. Addison loves to be outdoors in God's marvelous creation, which inspired the idea for this book.

Printed in the United States
by Baker & Taylor Publisher Services